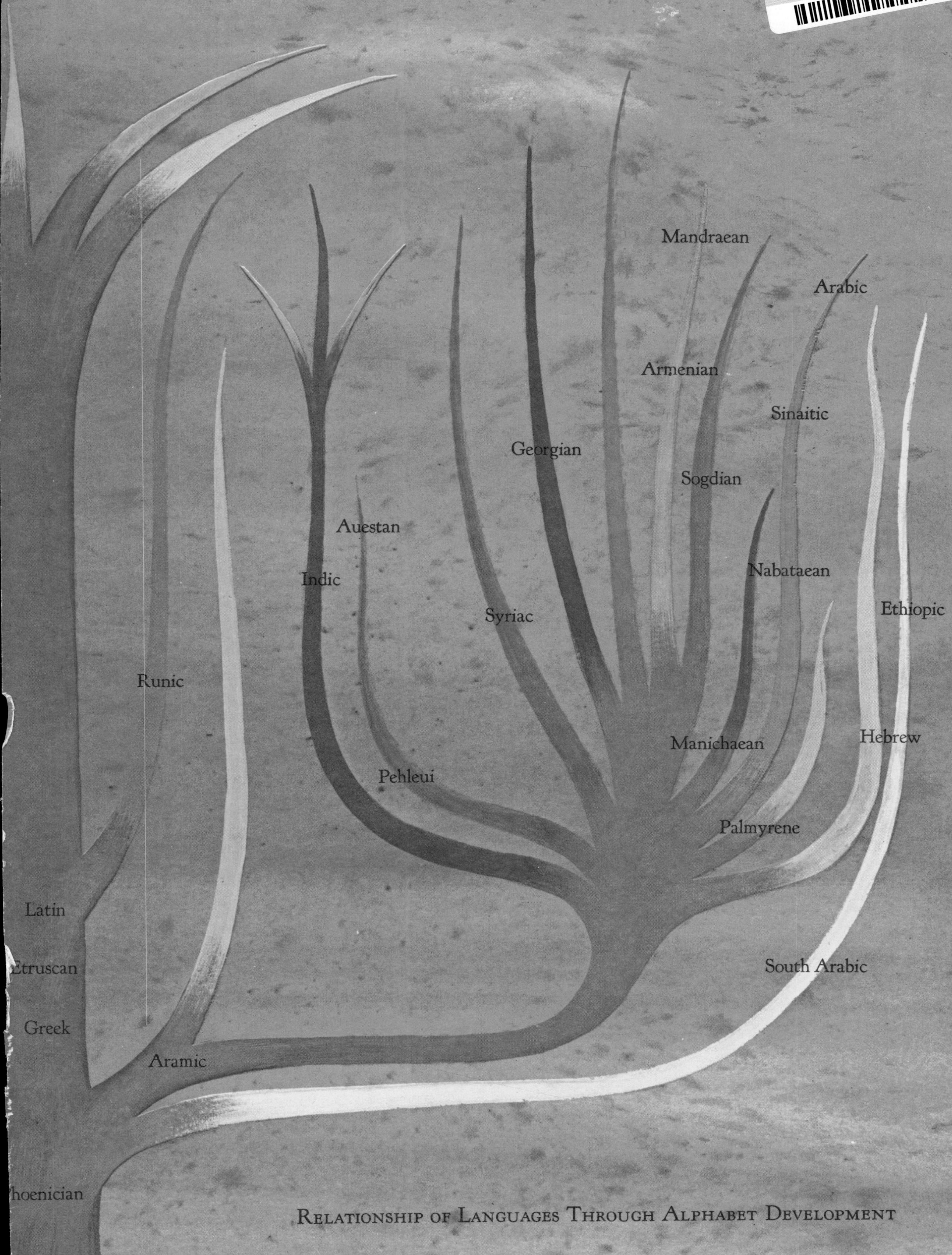

RELATIONSHIP OF LANGUAGES THROUGH ALPHABET DEVELOPMENT

HOW OUR ALPHABET GREW

The History of the Alphabet

Written and Illustrated by William Dugan

WORLD DISTRIBUTORS

Contents

Published in Great Britain by World Distributors (Manchester) Limited.
A Member of the Pentos Group, P.O. Box 111, 12 Lever Street, Manchester M60 1TS,
by arrangement with Western Publishing Company, Inc., Racine, Wisconsin, U.S.A.

Printed in Spain by EVA.
D. L. : BI 1167-1977

The Letters We Use

MESSAGES IN PICTURES

This is an A. I know it and you know it. Doesn't everyone?

Not quite! To most of the people of China, for example, the sign we call A means nothing. Although their writing system is a complicated one, it is not based on our alphabet—or on any other. You will understand the reason for this strange fact as you read on.

Alphabets did not always exist, nor did writing. But very early in his history, man felt the need of some means of putting down his thoughts, of making notes for himself and for others, of sending messages to friends and enemies. He needed to leave, for the members of his tribe, such messages as, "This is a great place for bison hunting"—important news for people who went hungry when the hunting was poor.

Man began to "write" by making sketches on the walls of caves. Then as time passed he discovered more advanced methods. First he made pictures of words, then pictures of ideas. Later came pictures of syllables, and last of all an alphabet, which is made up of symbols for the sounds we use in speaking. This process, from wall scratches to alphabet, took thousands of years and the talents and imaginations of great numbers of people.

Most of the steps that led to the development of an alphabet are still being used, as we shall see, for man never throws away anything that he has found useful.

HOW ALPHABETS GREW

The book you are about to read will tell the story of the growth of our alphabet, the Roman, which is only one of the 50 still in use. It is named after the Romans. who put it together more than 2500 years ago. But the Romans were great borrowers, and their alphabet was based on the work of others. Today it is more widely used than any other, for the Roman alphabet is employed by about a thousand million people.

Word Language and Sign Language

Man is the only creature on earth who can express his thoughts in words, and some scientists think he began to speak about 34,000 years ago. Others believe that human language has been in use for only half that time. Which group is right we may never know, for the men who lived so long ago had no way of leaving records.

Before our ancestors learned to talk, they probably let others know their thoughts as a baby does. It is likely that they grunted, made gestures, and showed their emotions by laughing, shouting, and scowling.

During man's long history, he found other ways of communicating that had no need of the spoken word. The ancient Greeks spread the news by signal fires, and American Indians sent up smoke signals.

Even today we "talk" without words when we clap our hands to tell actors and other performers, "We like your work."

All of us use gestures as a way of talking.

We wave to bid good-bye.

We put out our arms to welcome our friends. We shake our heads to say "No."

But gestures are especially important in the work of policemen and sports officials. Traffic officers use hand signals to tell riders to go, stop, pull over, and so on. Umpires and referees also signal during games to tell team members the results of various moves.

The American Indian developed a whole language made up of gestures. Often, members of one tribe did not understand the languages of other tribes, but they were able to converse by using hand signals.

Messages in Sticks and Stones

MEMORY AIDS FOR PRIMITIVE MAN

Thirty-five thousand years ago, before man discovered how to use words, he had no towns and had erected no buildings. He had no domestic animals, no boats, and not even carts, for no one had yet thought of the wheel.

At that time, man was a hunter who lived in caves. His children had no need to attend school, for there was no reading or writing to be learned. But young people were taught skills that were important to their way of life: making tools from stones, building fires, hunting, and perhaps their tribe's system of sending messages, and of counting.

Even after man learned to talk, his life was still simple, but he needed a memory aid. Perhaps he wanted to remember to do something or to recall a fact.

10

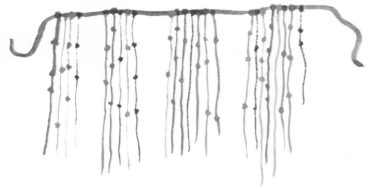

A Peruvian quipu

For a memory aid, the Incas of Peru used a *quipu*. As the picture above shows, this was made of a main cord from which hung smaller knotted cords of various colours. Each colour had its own meaning.

Quipus were used in counting, sending messages, and recording facts and events. The ancient Chinese, West African, and Australian natives used notched sticks and knotted ropes for the same purposes.

Notched message stick

The Zulus of Africa have a system of coloured beads that convey meaning. For example, a yellow bead means, "I am jealous"; a brown means, "Wish I were with you".

A Zulu girl wearing message beads

A Moon Calendar

Just recently other forms of memory aids have come to light—small pieces of bone, antler, and stone on which appear strange scratches and holes that were certainly made by human beings. Many people thought the markings were decorations, but others believed they served some useful purpose.

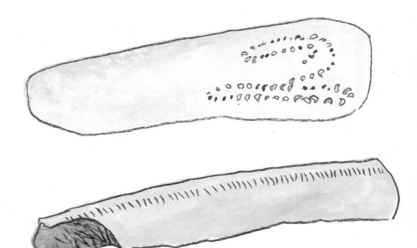

Primitive astronomers watched the skies and scratched on pieces of stone and bone what they had learned about the phases of the moon.

It was Alexander Marshack, a scientist, who suggested that these objects were moon calendars. To learn what tools had been used on the pieces of bone and stone, Mr. Marshack had large photographs made of the scratches and holes, for every tool leaves distinctive markings on any object it cuts.

Using the photographs, he was able to show that as many as 24 different tools had been used by primitive man to mark a single piece. If the scratches were only decorations, Mr. Marshack thought, no more than two or three tools would have been used. The use of so many tools indicated that the markings were made over a long period of time.

By comparing the markings, he concluded that the pieces were lunar calendars, used to record the phases of the moon from new moon to full moon, a period of almost a month. But why early man wanted such calendars, no one knows with certainty.

Cave Drawings

MAN THE TOOLMAKER

Primitive man made tools for many purposes; one of them was used to make scratches on the walls of caves and on bones, perhaps as a way of counting. As man gained more control of his scratches, he realised that he could form them in a variety of shapes.

Can you imagine the excitement of the first human who, more than 20,000 years ago, made an animal drawing? Think of his delight as he saw a likeness taking shape under his hands!

12

That first crude drawing was a primitive form of art, but it was also the first of the numberless steps that would lead, many centuries later, to writing and to an alphabet.

It is believed that the earliest drawings were made on bone, which is fairly soft, but eventually the hard walls of caves were decorated with the pictures of such animals as bison, goats, and reindeer.

The drawings, even those done on bone, were tinted with colours that had probably been made from such minerals as ochre and from the charcoal left from wood fires. It is believed the colours were mixed with animal fat and then blown through bone tubes onto walls. Crayons, too, may have been made from this mixture.

WHY DID THE CAVEMAN DRAW?

Most likely, cave pictures were used for religious ceremonies before and after the hunt. Perhaps man believed that making pictures of animals gave him power over them. Some drawings may even have been made by people who just liked to create things. We can only guess. But such drawings have been found on every continent, and among people in all parts of the world.

The two sketches on this page are cave drawings of wild horses, which were hunted by primitive man.

13

The Amazing Cave at Altamira

Stone Age Man, who lived more than 10,000 years ago, was quite a remarkable creature. He had not yet learned to work metals, but he was able to make fine tools from bone, horn, and stone. Neither did he know how to raise cattle for food or to grow his own crops, and so for his food he had to hunt such animals as reindeer, wild oxen and horses, woolly rhinoceroses, and mammoths. These are the animals he drew with such skill on the walls of dark caves, deep inside the earth.

The cave paintings of Stone Age artists may still be seen today, and one of the most famous is at Altamira in Spain. It was discovered about a hundred years ago by a man who went into a cave with his five-year-old granddaughter Maria to search for Stone Age relics. The little girl grew bored after a while and wandered deeper into the cave. Suddenly her grandfather heard her cry, "Bulls! Bulls!"

When he rushed to her, Maria pointed up at the walls. Her grandfather raised his lantern, glanced upwards, and saw there large coloured drawings of bison and other animals. He and little Maria had discovered the now famous grotto of Altamira and its beautiful art work.

The first cave drawings were animal portraits, that is, pictures of animals standing quietly. Sometimes the drawings showed only a head and sometimes the whole animal. No action was ever pictured in those early drawings.

Storytelling Pictures

Thing Pictures

The drawing of moving creatures was a major step forward in the history of writing; for the first time man was telling a story. The artist was using a *pictograph*—a "thing picture"—to say, "Today I saw a horse running!"

At first animals were the subjects of all of man's drawings, but after a time likenesses of man himself began to appear. Those early portraits of

Animal Pictures

But a day came when someone drew an animal in motion. Perhaps the artist had taken part in a hunt and watched a horse running across a plain. Or perhaps he had come upon two animals fighting. When he returned to his cave, he made a picture of what he had seen—a horse running or two animals fighting.

human beings were also motionless. But eventually they too began to show movement.

Now picture stories could be told about the hunt. A running horse could be followed by a running man, and it would seem to say, "I chased a horse."

When one of our cave-dwelling ancestors wanted to say *man* in a pictograph, he had only to draw a figure like this:

DRAWINGS THAT TOLD THE NEWS

Man had a reason for drawing in so simple a way. To make a careful picture of each person or object mentioned in even the briefest story would have taken too much time. If the artist wanted to say *buffalo*, it might look like this:

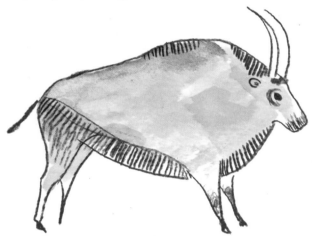

Suppose a cave dweller wanted to say, "Three hunters hunted and killed ten buffalo." How would he say *hunter*? A simple human figure would say only *man*.

Here is what the artist probably did. He drew a stick figure for *man*, but then inserted a spear in the man's hand. Now the figure said *hunter*.

For *ten buffalo*, the artist would draw a single buffalo and then make ten marks beneath it.

He could then show three hunters in pursuit of ten buffalo, as in the above picture.

Next he would show the hunters thrusting their spears into the buffalo.

With these two pictures he would be saying, "Three hunters hunted and killed ten buffalo."

A Hunting Trip

Here is a famous pictograph of a hunting trip in Alaska. The picture on page 19 shows how it might have been written had the artist been trying to make it look real. The picture on page 18 shows the way it was actually written with easy-to-make symbols. It is easy to see how much faster it would be to write with the use of symbols.

This is the story:

1) The storyteller points to himself, meaning, I. The other hand is saying, "Went away."

2) "I travelled by boat." The paddle shows how he travelled.

3) "I had one night's sleep." This is a way of telling that he travelled for only one day.

4) "I reached an island where there were two huts."

5) "I went away again."

6) "I came to another island."

7) "I spent two nights on this island."

8) "I got a harpoon."

9) "I saw a sea lion."

10) "I hunted the sea lion."

11) "I travelled by boat again with another person."

12) "I returned home."

Easy-to-Read Pictographs

To understand pictographic writing, it is not necessary for the reader to know the writer's language. Pictographs are not based on words, but on the recognition of drawings of people, animals, and objects.

1. 2. 3. 4.
5. 6. 7. 8.
9. 10. 11. 12.

A pictograph of a caribou

IDEA PICTURES

After early man developed the pictograph, he advanced another step. Sometimes he would draw a picture of one thing to mean something else. A spear would not mean *spear* but *enemy.*

A bow and arrow might mean *to hunt.*

Peace might be shown like this, for no one could fight with a broken spear!

Such idea pictures are called *ideograms.*

Ideograms are still used, though we are far from primitive man. The heart pierced by an arrow that you see on Valentine's Day cards means *love,* and two clasped hands are a sign of *friendship.*

ACTION WORDS IN PICTURES

Suppose someone wanted to write the verb *to drink*. He couldn't draw *to drink*, could he? He might make a drawing of someone drinking, but that would take too long.

In early picture writing, the writers got around this problem by putting two things together. They combined pictures of two objects, which together had a different meaning than either one had by itself. They would say *to drink* by showing water flowing across a pair of lips.

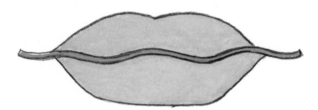

It's fun for us now to try to work out the meaning of pictographs and ideograms, but as a system of writing they weren't very satisfactory. For one thing, different artists drew the same things in different ways.

A MIXED-UP MESSAGE

Picture writing presented a second difficulty: Two people reading the same picture story might interpret it differently. About 550 B.C., after a Persian general named Darius had marched his army into the land of the Scythians, he received a pictographic message from the enemy.

Darius thought the letter announced that the Scythians, frightened by his army, had all run away. Imagine his surprise when that night they attacked his camp.

Darius had misread the message. Actually it had warned the Persians to leave the land of the Scythians or be attacked.

But usually pictographs worked well, for the daily life of long ago was simple, and much less complicated than the life of today. As more and more inventions came along and people's activities grew more varied, a much greater number of words were needed to describe those inventions and activities.

Pictographs would not do at all as a writing system for modern man. To write English we would have to learn 600 thousand symbols, instead of the 26 letters of our alphabet.

PICTURES OR LETTERS

In a pictographic system of writing, a new symbol would have to be invented for each new word that came into the language. For instance, *astronaut* is a fairly new word. We can spell it by using some of our 26 letters. But if we wrote as the Chinese do, we would have to invent a completely new character for the word.

The Scythian attack on the army of Darius the Persian

20

Symbols Everyone Can Read

Today we still use symbols to convey messages. A brand on the flank of a cow means, "This animal belongs to Farmer So and So."

Stores dealing in certain goods or services often have picture signs hanging outside.

A key means, "We make keys."

A watch means, "We sell and repair clocks and watches."

A red and white striped pole means, "Barber's Shop."

A symbol we all know is the American flag. When anyone sees it, he thinks not of a mere piece of cloth with some stars and stripes on it, but of the entire United States.

Sound Pictures

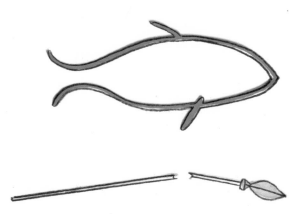

THE REBUS

Early man used symbols for things, such as *fish,* or ideas, such as *peace.*

But one day someone had a clever idea—he would write down the sounds he made when he spoke. That is what we do in English today. When a person sees the word *car,* he recognises it, but the word doesn't look like the picture of a motor car. Yet it is a picture in a way. It is a picture of a sound—the sound of the word *car.*

How did the first man who wrote the picture of a sound go about it? Perhaps it was an accident. Or perhaps the first person to write such a sound did so as a joke. It would work this way:

Suppose that you, whenever you wanted to write the word *I,* were to draw the picture of an eye, instead.

That would be fun, wouldn't it? But you would also have drawn the picture of a sound. Gradually it would become accepted that this picture no longer meant *eye,* an organ of vision, but *I,* a person.

22

Pictures that are used to represent sounds are called *phonograms,* from two Greek words meaning *voice* and *writing.*

Today you can still see this kind of picture story in children's books and magazines. Such a story is a puzzle that uses pictures instead of words, and is called a rebus. The pictures above are rebuses.

The two pictures above are rebuses. Can you read them? If not, their meanings are given below.

The Sumerians

THE LAND OF SUMER

Many scholars believe that the Sumerians were the developers of a system of writing based on sound pictures. Not a great deal is known about these people. In fact, no one knew they had even existed until about a hundred years ago, and the Babylonians were given credit for the writing system that was probably a Sumerian invention.

BETWEEN THE RIVERS

But we now know that about 5000 years ago these remarkable people settled along the Tigris and Euphrates rivers, at the head of the Persian Gulf, in an area called Mesopotamia. This land, about a thousand miles east of present-day Israel, was a dismal place. The plains of the two rivers contained neither trees nor minerals, and very little rain ever fell.

Here the Sumerians built the first great advanced civilization. It was in their city of Ur that Abraham, the Father of the Hebrews, was born, and where he lived until he led his family on their long journey to the land of Canaan.

The Sumerians used the wheel, the plough, and the sailboat. They learned to make baked-clay brick and to build beautifully decorated houses, temples, and cities. They were skilful weavers of woollen fabrics, and they made objects—both beautiful and useful—of metals from foreign lands.

With the river waters, the Sumerians irrigated their land and became successful farmers. They developed law and government.

WORD PICTURES ON CLAY

When large numbers of people live together in cities, as the Sumerians did, they exchange goods, and must keep records of all kinds. Since the land

of the Sumerians contained no rock or wood on which to write, they had to search for another writing material. It did not take these resourceful people long to discover that clay from the river bed made a good enough surface if it were used while still soft and moist.

In the beginning a number of tools were employed to mark the clay with pictographs, and many drawings contained both straight and curved lines.

Here are some early Sumerian pictographs. Can you guess what they mean?

You were right if you said *bird, fish, ox,* and *grain.*

Eventually these pictographs developed into more complicated forms. This drawing appears to be a foot, but it meant *to stand* or *to walk.*

A Sumerian stone figurine. Such figures are believed to have represented gods.

25

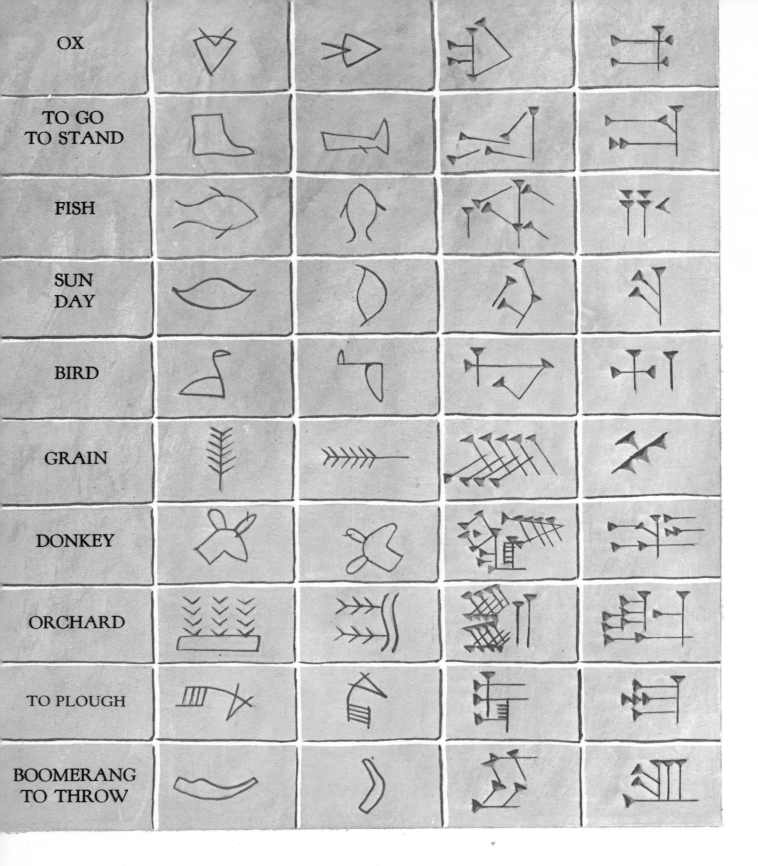

OX			
TO GO TO STAND			
FISH			
SUN DAY			
BIRD			
GRAIN			
DONKEY			
ORCHARD			
TO PLOUGH			
BOOMERANG TO THROW			

WEDGE-SHAPED WRITING

Soon the Sumerians found that it was time-consuming for a writer to change from one tool to another every time he wanted to make a different kind of line. The scribes, or writers, then decided to use only a single tool called a *stylus*. This was a reed—a kind of grass—with a triangular tip.

When pressed into wet clay, the stylus made a wedge shape, and so the writing done with it is called *cuneiform,* which means *wedge-shaped* in Latin.

After the writing on the tablet was finished, it was baked in the sun or in a potter's oven, and became very hard. Great numbers of such tablets have been found, and are still being unearthed today.

The earliest cuneiform writings date back to

This chart shows how Sumerian writing developed from pictures in column 1 on the left to the symbols shown in the column on the far right. This development took place over a long period of time.

3500 B.C. Many tablets are business contracts, lists, receipts, and accounts. Others are of a legal nature, such as wills, adoptions, and court decisions. Some are letters. Others are grammars of the lost Sumerian language.

On some of the tablets Sumerian epics, hymns, proverbs, and "words of wisdom" are inscribed. They provide the oldest literature ever found in large quantities.

FROM LEFT TO RIGHT

The writing on the oldest tablets began in the upper right corner and moved down the tablet from top to bottom, with all the symbols facing to the right, as the picture shows. Later, the tablets were turned so that they rested on the left edge and the writing was done from left to right, thus:

No one knows with certainty the reason for the change, but it was probably easier to work that way. When a right-handed person writes as the Sumerians originally did, his arm tends to smear the letters as he moves across from right to left.

Curves were so hard to make with the stylus that they gradually disappeared from cuneiform writing. With the placing of the symbols on their backs, the original pictures became harder to recognise.

THE MARKS OF CUNEIFORM

Finally, the scribes stopped trying to make symbols look like "thing pictures" and simplified their drawings even more. In the end, all the symbols were made up of only four marks, plus a fifth made with the top of the stylus.

On the opposite page look for the word *fish.* There you can see how the character for *fish* developed from the pictograph, which looks like a fish, to the final symbol, which looks like nothing in nature.

SYLLABLE PICTURES

The final symbols of cuneiform were not letters, although there were characters for the vowels a, e, i, and u. The other characters represented syllables, combinations of more than one sound, and were part of a form of writing called *syllabary.*

A syllable is one sound or a combination of sounds which make up a single effort of the voice. The word *number,* for example, has two syllables: *num* and *ber.*

Syllabary writing was a great improvement on the pictograph, but it was still not an alphabet because symbols of an alphabet stand for single sounds, not syllables. Although the Sumerians had made great advances in the history of writing, they left the discovery of a true alphabet to others.

When, ages after the Sumerians had disappeared, their cuneiform tablets were found, reading them presented a problem, for their language was no longer spoken anywhere on the earth. But scientists, working from the idea that certain signs were the names of kings, were, after many years and much hard work, able to decipher the meaning of the tablets.

THE SPREAD OF CUNEIFORM

The cuneiform method of writing was so efficient that it was soon adopted by other people who dwelt in Mesopotamia. Among those who borrowed from the Sumerian syllabary of about 500 characters were the Babylonians and Assyrians, both great powers in the ancient world.

The Egyptians

ALONG THE NILE

At the time the Sumerians were developing their culture, there lived, 1000 miles to the west in the valley of Africa's Nile River, a people we know as the Egyptians. Many scholars believe that the Egyptian civilization came into being long before the Sumerians settled in Mesopotamia, and that it continued long after the Sumerians had been displaced by others.

The first Egyptians were probably desert tribes who settled along the river. They farmed the land, raised domestic animals, and even grew flax and wove linen. They learned to make tools and copper weapons, and invented a calendar. About 5000 years ago, they united into one nation ruled by a pharaoh, or king, whom they believed to be a god.

THE PYRAMIDS

Among the accomplishments of the Egyptians was engineering, of which their pyramids stand as

The temple at Abu Simbel on the Nile River. Built on a rocky hillside more than 3200 years ago, this temple was a monument to Rameses II, a Pharaoh who thought himself a god. In 1965-66, rising water caused by the new Aswan Dam forced the removal of the temple to higher ground.

A portrait bust of Queen Nefertiti, wife of the Pharaoh Iknaton. Nefertiti's name means "The beautiful one has come."

evidence. In the pyramids, built as tombs for the pharaohs, archaeologists have found much of what is known about Egyptian civilization.

The Pyramids can tell us much about the Egyptians, for they believed the Pharaoh would need in the next world the things he used on earth. For this reason the people put into the pyramids such things as chairs, tables, and chests—many of them beautifully carved and covered with gold and jewels. There were also daggers and other weapons, game boards, jewellery, clothing, jars of oil, and other articles. On the walls of some inner rooms, prayers and hymns were written in beautiful characters. All these help us to know how the Egyptians lived.

HIEROGLYPHICS

In the beginning, *hieroglyphics,* as the Egyptian writing symbols are called, were carved or painted on stone by priests only. (*Hieroglyphics* means priest-writing.) In this writing, pictographs were used, but it also included such other forms of writing as ideograms and sound-pictures. In addition, there were over 75 symbols for pairs of consonants (consonants are letters that are not vowels); no vowels were represented in hieroglyphics.

AN UNFINISHED ALPHABET

To all these symbols, the Egyptians added 24 that represented the sounds of single consonants. Had the Egyptians used their 24 letters and disposed of their other forms of writing, they would have had a real alphabet. But they had great respect for their ancestors and a love for things of the past. Even after they had enough letters to spell out the words of their language, they continued to use the old pictographs and ideograms.

Hieroglyphics were harder to learn than our alphabet because there were so many of them. The few men who learned to write the hieroglyphics were called *scribes,* and they held honoured positions in Egyptian society.

This painting found on the walls of an Egyptian tomb shows a man
and his wife harvesting grain and making offerings to the gods.
Hieroglyphics can be seen in the three upper parts of the picture.
Such wall paintings also add to our knowledge of Egyptian life.

Animals and birds are an important part of hieroglyphics. At first they may have been used as the symbols of various tribes, a practice similar to one we use today when we call our sports teams *The Eagles, The Bears, The Lions,* and so on.

Among the Egyptians, the tribal animals gradually began to take on religious meanings. A god in their writing was often shown as part animal. The sun god, Ra, for example, had the head of a hawk.

In early hieroglyphics, animal pictures were used as pictographs. A drawing of an eagle means *eagle*.

Later, certain animal pictures became idea-pictures. An eagle with a man's face no longer meant *eagle;* it became the symbol for *soul*.

Later still, animal pictures were used to represent letters, and the eagle became a symbol for the sound of A.

In an even later form of writing, the eagle no longer looked like an animal at all but took on the shape of a real letter.

The pictures in the first column show that as the Egyptians developed their writing system, the symbols became more and more simple. Notice how plain the final sign for A is in comparison with the sign that precedes it.

These changes took place because scribes grew less concerned with the beauty of their writings, and more concerned with stating a message as quickly as possible.

Imagine how dull and time-consuming it would be if every time we wanted to write an A, we had to draw an eagle! Or suppose we were to use a lion for the letter L and a dinosaur for D. Writing a short note would take forever.

Not all Egyptian symbols were pictures of animals. Here are some that represented ordinary things:

They say *bowl, hand, leaf, tongs,* and *weapon*.

The Egyptian sign for *mouth* (Ro in Egyptian) later became the letter R.

The symbol for *water* (Nu) was finally used to represent the sound of our letter N.

33

How Papyrus Was Made

Many of the hieroglyphics were carved in stone and painted on walls, but the Egyptians had also developed a fine writing material called *papyrus,* so named because it was made from the papyrus plant, a swamp grass. Our word *paper* comes from *papyrus.*

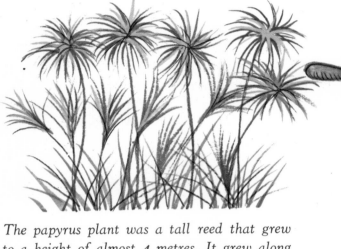

The papyrus plant was a tall reed that grew to a height of almost 4 metres. It grew along the banks of the Nile and in the wet grounds of the river's delta. Papyrus plants were the "bulrushes" of the Bible story about the infant Moses.

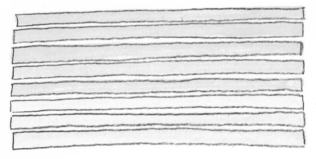

Above: As a first step in making papyrus plants into paper, the strips were laid out in rows.

Below: A second row of strips were laid across the first.

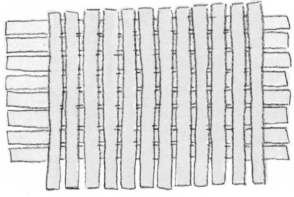

This plant was also used by the Egyptians for food and clothing, as well as for such things as rope and sails.

In preparing papyrus for writing, the pith was removed and the stalk cut into thin strips. After these were placed side by side, they were covered with muddy river water or with flour paste. Other strips were then placed on top of this layer, at right angles to the first strips.

A roll of papyrus is ready for the scribe to begin his writing.

The entire mixture was hammered into a thin sheet and dried in the sun. Finally it was polished with ivory or a shell. The sheets, which varied in width from 15 cm in earlier times to 45 cm later on, were then glued together to form rolls, some of which were over a hundred feet long.

The use of papyrus was a great improvement over such earlier writing materials as basalt, granite, sandstone, wood, and plaster. It could be made in either large or small sheets, and was easy to carry about.

Eventually, papyrus became the chief writing material of much of the ancient world, and was in use for about 4000 years. As late as the 11th century, it was still in use in parts of Europe.

The oldest papyrus document still in existence was written about 4000 years ago. How is it possible for us to read these ancient writings?

Making papyrus. In the distance a worker gathers the reed from the marshes. Another worker carries the papyrus to the hut. Inside the building, a third man is placing one row of strips across another. In the foreground finished sheets are being put out to dry in the sun.

Digging for the Past

We have been given the answer by *archaeologists,* students of the remains of old cultures. An archaeologist may decide, after a great deal of study and research, that a very old city once stood at a certain place. Going there, he will dig with great care, hoping to uncover the remains of the ancient city. If he has been a good detective, he will find what he is seeking, together with such remains of long-dead civilizations as weapons, carvings, and pottery.

It was archaeologists who learned to read Egyptian hieroglyphics. Because of a remarkable accident, their task was somewhat less complicated than that of the archaeologists who deciphered the Sumerians' cuneiform. Here is what happened:

About 170 years ago, Napoleon Bonaparte, leading a French army, fought in Egypt. He lost the battle, but something good came from the campaign. Near a place called Rosetta, one of his men discovered, partly buried in the earth, a piece of black basalt rock that was covered with strange writing. With this find began a study of Egyptian hieroglyphics that continues today.

The Rosetta Stone

On the Rosetta Stone, as the piece of basalt was called, three columns of writing had been scratched. The first two were hieroglyphics and another form of Egyptian writing, but the third column was written in Greek, a language which many educated people of that time could read.

Believing that all the columns told the same story, the archaeologists thought that by using the Greek text as a key, they might be able to interpret the two other columns. Although this would appear to be a fairly easy task, it took many scholars 40 years to finish it. But when we remember that men had been trying in vain to read Egyptian heiroglyphics since the 16th century, those 40 years were not a very long time.

The Rosetta Stone, with two forms of Egyptian writing at the top and the Greek inscription beneath them.

Jean Francois Champollion

The man who did the most important work in uncovering the mysteries of the Rosetta Stone was a Frenchman, Jean Francois Champollion, who had been interested in hieroglyphics since his boyhood. With great excitement, he noticed that in the Egyptian writing there were ovals that contained symbols. When later he came upon an obelisk, a tall Egyptian stone monument, he saw that it was marked with similar ovals, and that on it, too, were hieroglyphics and Greek writing.

Champollion wondered whether the ovals contained the names of kings and queens because *Ptolemy,* a king, and *Cleopatra,* were spelled out in the Greek writing on both the obelisk and the Rosetta Stone. Choosing two of the ovals for closer study, he compared those on both monuments. They were quite similar.

Many of the same letters appeared in both names. By comparing those on the stone and on the obelisk, Champollion was able to identify 13 symbols.

With these letters as a start, he worked out other ovals, and one by one he learned the meanings of new characters.

Gradually he was able to identify these same symbols in other parts of the stone and thus to discover words, then parts of sentences, and finally whole sentences.

Champollion spent most of his life trying to solve the meaning of the hieroglyphics on the Rosetta Stone, but he died before finishing his task. However, he had found the key which made it possible for others to complete what he had begun. It was Champollion who had unlocked the mysteries of Egyptian writing.

The Cleopatra oval pictured below shows that many kinds of writings were used in Egyptian hieroglyphics. Most of the symbols are letters, but three represent whole words: *divine, female,* and *royalty.*

Hieratic Writing

Originally the hieroglyphics were carved on stone or wood, but for everyday use, they were written with brush and pen, and could be formed much more quickly than letters could be carved on hard material. As time went on, these rapidly written letters gradually changed in appearance, and became a form of writing called *hieratic* because it had originally been used by priests for religious books.

But hieratic was also used in trade and wherever speed rather than beauty was needed. This form of writing was based on hieroglyphics, but as time went on it grew harder and harder to see any resemblance between the two.

This Oval contains the hieroglyphic symbols that made up Cleopatra's name.

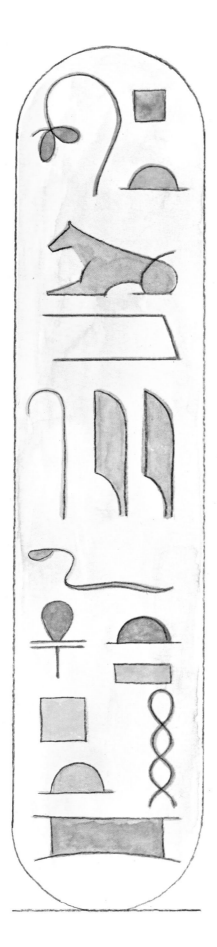

The Oval in which Ptolemy's name was spelled out in hieroglyphics.

DEMOTIC WRITING

Much later, probably in the seventh century B.C., an even simpler form of writing was developed by the common people for the writing of business records, bills, and so on. But this *demotic* writing, as it was called, eventually came into use throughout Egypt for all kinds of written work.

Both hieratic and demotic were faster to write than were hieroglyphics, but they were much less beautiful. Because of this and because of their love for old forms, the Egyptians continued to use hieroglyphics on their monuments and in important documents.

An example of hieratic writing. Although this script was fast and efficient, it was not as decorative as hieroglyphics.

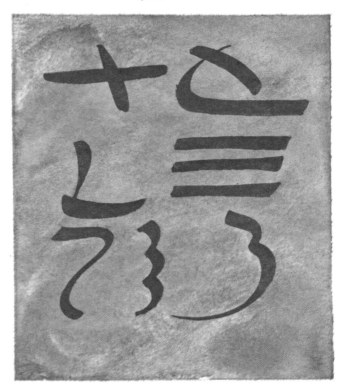

The Phoenicians

INVENTORS OF THE ALPHABET

The Egyptians were a great people who developed writing to a high degree. But, as we have seen, they never developed a true alphabet. Who did then?

Most archaeologists believe that the first real alphabet was the work of the Phoenicians, a Semitic people who lived on the Mediterranean coast just north of present-day Israel. They called themselves "Canaanites"; the name "Phoenicians" was given to them much later by the Greeks.

The Phoenicians, or Canaanites, were merchants, businessmen, and skilful sailors. Their city of Tyre, the Bible tells us, traded throughout the Mediterranean Sea in silver, iron, lead, tin, brass, and copper. It also marketed lambs, rams, goats, horses, and mules, and such luxury items as emeralds, coral, agate, ivory, linen, spices, and "royal-purple" dyes.

Another important Phoenician city was named *Byblos* by the Greeks from their word for papyrus, an important article of trade in Byblos. In turn, our English word *Bible* comes from the city's name.

Phoenician ships travelled as far west as Britian where they bought tin. They may have even sailed around Africa.

BORROWED WRITING

No one is quite certain about how the Phoenicians developed their alphabet. Like most people, they first used pictographs. Then, when they traded with Egypt, they may have become acquainted with the hieroglyphics in use there. Indeed, there are some who think it was from the Egyptians that the Phoenicians borrowed the symbols for the first

A Phoenician ship, powered by oarsmen and the wind. Phoenician sailors were skilful and brave men who were the first to dare to sail at night, using the North Star as a guide. So great was their reputation as seamen that their ships and crews were used in the navies of other countries.

alphabet, as you will read below. But others believe the Phoenician characters were influenced by the writing of their Semitic neighbours or by the Sumerians or the Minoan people of Crete.

Our Alphabet's Ancestor

Other alphabets were being worked out by other Semitic-speaking people at about the same time. But the Phoenicians have an especially important place in our story, for it was their alphabet that was passed along to the Greeks, who handed it on to the Romans, who in turn gave it to us for use in books like the one you are reading.

Some stones and tablets from as far back as 1800 B.C. tell us what little we know about the growth of the Phoenician writing system. One such stone, found at Byblos, leads us to believe that the Phoenicians first used a syllabary of about 80 characters.

Another tiny tablet, found at the site of Ugarit, contains the alphabet of 30 letters used by the Phoenicians 2500 years ago. This tablet is the oldest record of a true alphabet in existence.

An Alphabet Without Vowels

The Egyptian writing system, with its great number of characters, was too complicated for the Phoenicians, and so they seem to have used some of the hieroglyphics to stand for sounds in their own language. It is believed they would take a character that represented some familiar object, such as an animal or a household object or a part of the body. Instead of using this character as a pictogram, they would then use it to represent only the first sound in the object's name.

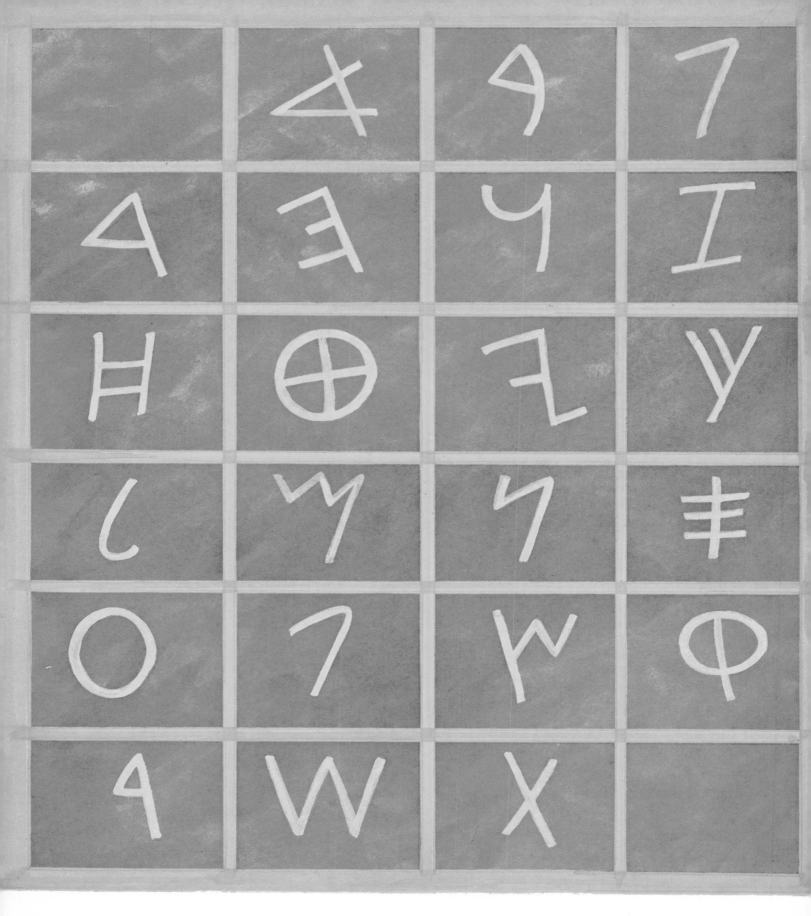

The Phoenician alphabet. These 22 characters were originally borrowed by the Greeks and passed on in altered form to the Romans.

For example, suppose we were going to make up a writing system as the Phoenicians seem to have done. We might draw a picture like this:

The picture would not mean *cat*, as in a pictogram, but the sound of the letter C. The same would be true if we were to draw a picture of a train. The picture would not mean *train*, but the sound of T.

In this system of ours, we would write the word *cat* like this for, like the Phoenicians, we wouldn't have any symbols for vowels:

If we were to make the picture of an apple to stand for our A, we would spell *cat* like this:

But, you may ask, wouldn't it be simpler to draw a cat if that is what you wanted to show? After all, everyone knows what a cat looks like! Then, instead of having to draw three pictures for the word *cat*, you would need only one.

But think of how long it would take to draw a picture that looked like a cat and not like some other animal. And how many people would have enough talent to do so?

Suppose, too, that the characters were changed to speed up the writing, as has happened in all writing. Do you think you would be able to recognise

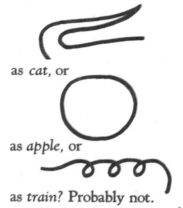

as *cat*, or

as *apple*, or

as *train*? Probably not.

Following a system like the imaginary one described above, as we believe the Phoenicians did, they were able to reduce their alphabet to 22 simple consonant characters. With these they could then write any word in their language.

WRITING IN CHINA

Compare this alphabet with that of the Chinese, whose characters at present number as many as 50,000!

The Chinese, once among the most advanced peoples on earth, were held back by their writing system. It was so complicated and difficult that very few of them learned to read and write. The printing of cheap books was almost impossible, and without them, there could be no public education of the poorer classes of people.

By contrast, the Phoenician system was easy to learn, even though they had no symbols for vowel sounds in their alphabet. This did not make reading as difficult as we might think, for we ourselves sometimes omit vowels in abbreviations. For example, we know at once that *pg.* is to be read as *page*. Try to read this sentence in which the vowels have been omitted: "Cn Jm rd tht bk?"

Of course, it says, "Can Jim read that book?"

A Greek soldier
and his war chariot.

The Greeks

Among the people with whom the Phoenicians traded were the inhabitants of a peninsula that extended into the Mediterranean Sea northwest of Egypt. They were the Greeks who had settled there about 3800 years ago and become farmers, growing barley and wheat, and raising grapes and olives. Later they made textiles, pottery, and metal products.

Living near the sea, they soon began to trade with other people. Their ships carried Greek products to various countries and returned with such things as grain and fish.

The Greeks became a great people and made valuable contributions to mankind, especially in art and literature. It was they who first tried the idea of democracy.

How the Alphabet Got Its Name

When they began to trade with the Phoenicians, the Greeks had no writing system, and so they probably used Phoenician letters to write the sounds of their own language. We believe this is so because they continued to call the letters by their Phoenician names. For instance, the Phoenicians called A *aleph,* the Semitic word for *ox-head,* and B *beth,* the Semitic word for *house.* The Greeks changed the names to *alpha* and *beta;* put together, these give us our word *alphabet.*

The Greeks borrowed nineteen Phoenician characters which, of course, were symbols for consonants, but the Greeks needed vowels to write their language. To get them, they used Phoenician symbols for sounds that are not used in Greek, and invented new ones, such as, Φ Χ Ψ Ω

In addition, the Greeks dropped the Phoenician letters for which they had no use. In the various city-states of Greece, people made local changes in the alphabet, but this caused confusion in such a small country, and in 403 B.C. the government of the Greek city of Athens adopted a 24-character alphabet. This is still in use among the people of modern Greece.

The Greeks had another important contribution to make to the art of writing. At that time they sometimes wrote from right to left, sometimes from left to right, sometimes up and down.

Now and then they wrote in what they called *boustrophedon,* a word that means *like an ox turning.* When an ox pulled a plough to the end of a field, it turned and pulled the plough in the opposite direction. This kind of writing would then go first from right to left and then from left to right. If we were to write in boustrophedon, it would look like this:

Greek boys went to school to learn the alphabet, reading, writing, and music.

Writing in more than one direction made reading difficult, and finally the Greeks decided to write always from left to right, as we do. That is why some characters which faced one way when they were Phoenician, such as Ⅎ, turned and faced the other way, ⴹ when they became Greek.

Some people, the Hebrews, for example, decided to write from right to left, and still do to this day.

But the Greeks left some problems to be solved later in history. For example, they used no spaces between words, no full stops, and no commas. They used only capital letters. Writing that way, here is how a sentence might appear:

WRITINGISEASYITISTHESPELLING-THATISHARD

Although the Greeks could, and often did, write with pen on papyrus, most of their writing which is still in existence was carved on stone. Such a carving—a very ancient one—looks like this:

5. Etruscans

6. Romans

4. Greeks

This map pictures the area in which the alpha-bet was born. The very beginnings were to the east—Sumer, Egypt, and Phoenicia. The alphabet then moved westward to Greece and Rome. From Rome, it finally spread throughout Europe.

The Etruscans

PEOPLE OF MYSTERY

To the Greeks, beauty was important in all things. They continued to work on the form and arrangement of letters until, over the centuries, they had made writing handsome for its own sake.

All that the Greeks learned about the art of writing was passed along to the Etruscans. Some 2800 years ago these people came to power in central Italy. Although little is known about them, historians believe they came from Asia Minor. Whatever their origin, it is almost certain that they learned their alphabet from the Greeks.

If we could read the thousands of examples of Etruscan writing, we could learn much more about them. But, even though their words are written in characters that look like Greek, only a very few of them can be read because their language has been lost.

But from the tombs of the Etruscans, which are filled with beautiful sculptures and wall paintings, we know they were clever builders and engineers who loved music, dancing, and festivals.

AN ETRUSCAN ALPHABET

We also know the order of their alphabet from a writing tablet found at Marsiliana in Italy. Perhaps to help some schoolboy's memory, the tablet had the alphabet written along its edge. It reads from right to left, and is inscribed with 22 Phoenician letters followed by four Greek letters.

This tablet is the oldest known example of Etruscan writing.

When the Etruscans borrowed the Greek letters, they did not add some characters and drop others, as the Greeks had done with the Phoenician alphabet. The Etruscans added letters needed to express the sounds of their language, but they kept all the Phoenician signs too. As a result, some of their sounds were represented by more than one letter.

This is confusing, but it is done today in our own language. For example, our letter C is pronounced with either a K sound, as in *coin,* or with an S sound, as in *circle.* Our Q is also given the sound of K, as in *quick.*

Thus, three letters, Q, K, and C are used for the sound of K. We could drop Q and C and never miss them. We might then spell *quick* as *kwick* and *coin* as *koin.*

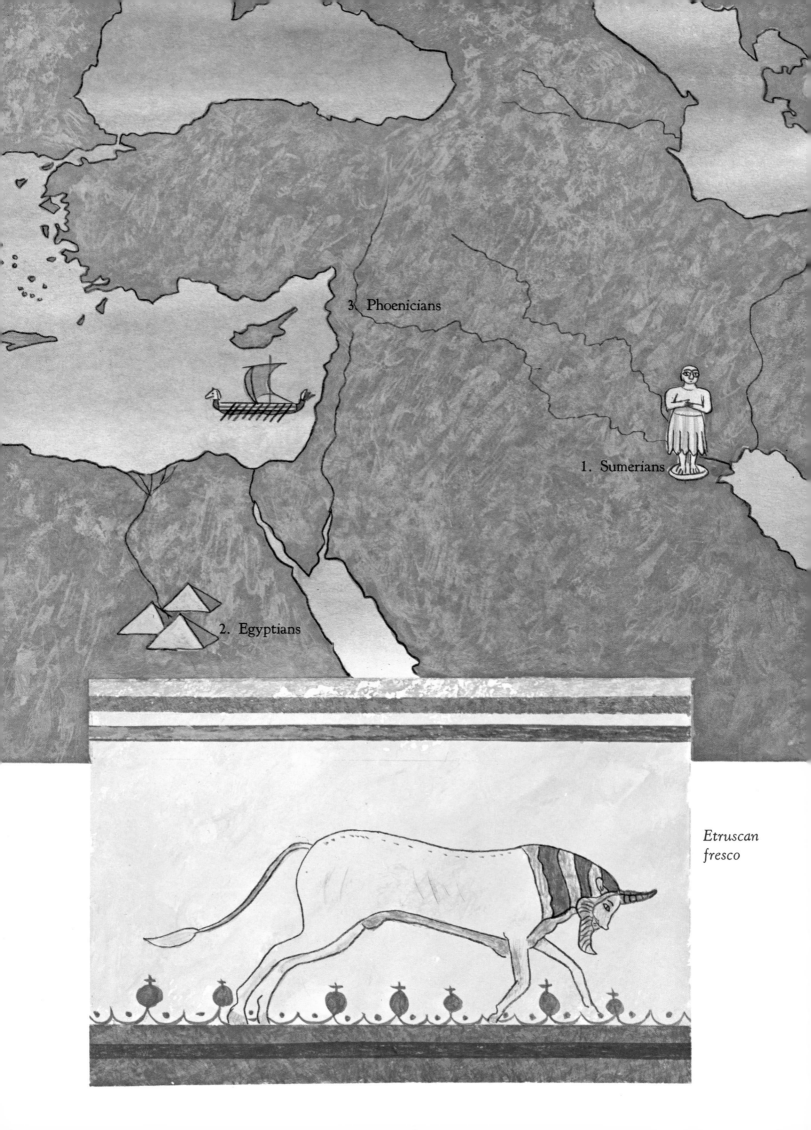

3. Phoenicians

1. Sumerians

2. Egyptians

*Etruscan
fresco*

The Romans

The Conquered Latins

In time, the Etruscans conquered the area north of Rome and ruled there for several hundred years. Among the tribes under their control were the Latins whose land, known as Latium, lay south of the Tiber River. The Latins built six villages on the seven hills that lay near the river, and as the small communities grew they became close enough to one another to form the one big city that is known to us as Rome.

The Latins had come from central Europe and settled as shepherds and farmers in the middle of what is now Italy. At first they lived in mud huts, each of which had a hole in its roof to let out the smoke of their fires.

Under the rule of the Etruscans, the Latins became acquainted with architecture and engineering. Then, probably during the seventh century B.C., they learned the alphabet then in use by the Etruscans.

Rome Grows Up

As the years passed, Rome became a powerful nation, conquering the Etruscans, as well as all the other tribes around them. Gradually their empire spread along the shores of the Mediterranean, and Rome became a wealthy city.

Romans no longer dwelt in one-roomed mud huts. Working men and their families lived in apartment buildings which were sometimes five storeys high, rather like some buildings in our cities today. The wealthier folk had handsome homes, with rooms built around gardens and courtyards, and fitted out with baths, toilets, and hot-air heating.

The sons of the wealthier Romans attended schools, but most girls were kept at home where they were educated by their mothers.

The Romans used 21 of the letters they had received from the Etruscans, and to these they made only one addition. This was the letter G, which was made from the C; it was officially accepted as part

48

A Roman chariot race

of the alphabet in the year 312 B.C. The new letter was used for the hard G sound which we hear at the beginning of *gate*.

The seventh letter of the Greek alphabet was Z, but the Romans thought they didn't need it and they put the new G in its place. When they discovered that the Z was needed after all, they put it at the end of the alphabet, where we find it today.

IMPROVEMENTS IN OUR ALPHABET

Other inventions of the Romans were thick and thin strokes in letters, and serifs, the thin lines at the bottom and top of strokes. Serifs were used because their straight lines gave a neatly finished look to the rough ends of letters.

These graceful Roman capitals were carefully designed and carved into the inscriptions on arches, statues, and other monuments which were erected in honour of emperors and to celebrate Rome's conquering armies.

The lines at the bottom of the A and those that extend to the left from the top and bottom of the B are serifs.

49

aвcde

What the Romans did is important to us because, except for J, U, and W, the alphabet they developed provides us with the capital letters we use today.

WRITING ON WAX

Among the Romans, everyday writing was done on a wooden tablet covered with a thin coating of black wax. A sharply pointed stylus was used to scratch through the wax to the light-coloured wood beneath. The scratchings would then appear as white characters against a black background.

After a scribe had finished writing his message, he could soften the wax with heat, smooth

ABCDEFG
OPQRSTV

THE LETTERS ON TRAJAN'S COLUMN

Eighteen hundred years ago, the Emperor Trajan set up a great column in Rome to celebrate his many victories. Winding around the column from the bottom to the top of its shaft are scenes in which there are the figures of 2500 men. But more important to us today is the base, whose simple, readable, dignified inscription is still being used as the model for beautiful lettering.

the surface, and write on his tablet again. It was a cheap material that could be used many, many times.

PAPYRUS ROLLS

For literary purposes, the Romans used papyrus, rolling the sheets on a stick. Such a roll, or scroll, was called a *volumen* by the Romans; from it we get our word *volume*. A volumen was usually

14m long and 25cm wide, but sometimes it was as much as 30m long. These rolls were used for official papers and documents.

Parchment and Vellum

Parchment was also used by the Romans as a writing surface. This material was made from the skins of calves, sheep, and goats; after the pelts had been washed, scraped, and rubbed with pumice, they were finished with chalk.

A finer grade of parchment, called *vellum,* was made from lamb, kid, and antelope skins. A metal pen was used to write on these surfaces.

With the use of parchment and pen, the shapes of the letters gradually changed. Because parchment was expensive, scribes tried to save space by writing their letters closer and closer together. The writing became smaller and the strokes thinner.

Cursive Writing

This style of writing, called *cursive,* was the ancestor of our small letters and our handwriting. In cursive writing, the pen was lifted less than in carved letters, and, as scribes wrote more and more speedily, many of the straight lines became curved. For instance, the Greek < gradually became the Roman C.

GHIKLMN VXYZ

The Roman alphabet on whose beautiful letters our capitals are based

A scribe writing on a wax tablet

51

UNCIAL LETTERS

Another style of writing that came into existence among the Romans was the *uncial*. These letters were influenced by cursive writing and were more rounded than formal capitals. Like the cursive too, uncial letters had lines that went above and below the rest of the letters.

Some of these began to look like our small letters, but to us the Roman uncials appear to be a combination of small letters and capitals.

copy had to be completely written by hand. But a man named Titus Pomponius found a partial solution to the problem: He taught a number of well-educated Greek slaves to become book copyists. One slave would be appointed to read to the others from a book that was to be copied, and they would then proceed to write down all that he said.

Thus it was possible to make a number of copies of a book at the same time. This system was used centuries later by the monks of the Middle Ages.

WRITING IN POMPEII

Examples of uncials written by ordinary people have been found in the ruins of Pompeii in Italy, a city that was buried under the ashes of a volcano almost 1900 years ago. When archaeologists uncovered it, they found on some walls the kind of message we see scrawled in public places today.

THE FIRST BOOKS

While the Roman Empire was still a world power, books began to be made. They were a decided advance because they took up less space than scrolls.

Although the Romans were becoming a nation of literary people, books were still rare, for each

Scribes doing copying work. One scribe reads from the original manuscript, while the others write down what he is saying.

In the early days of Rome, most of the books that reached the city were spoils of war and went into the collections of generals and men of wealth. But later, when people began to give more time to learning, Cicero and others who truly loved books began to collect them seriously. One man named Tyrannion owned 30,000 volumes—a huge library when we remember that each book was hand-written in those days before the printing press.

Then Julius Caesar had an idea: he would open a library where all the people might come to read. But nothing came of the idea until around 30 B.C., when Asinius Pollio opened Rome's first public library. The idea became so popular that many Roman emperors—among them Augustus, Vespasian, and Hadrian—also built public libraries. It is said that before the fall of Rome there were 28 of them in the city.

An uncial alphabet

To the West with the Alphabet

PATRICK IN IRELAND

About four centuries after Christ, a missionary named Saccath was sent to Ireland to bring Christianity to its people. He was made a bishop and given the name of Patricius, which means *noble*. We know him now as St. Patrick.

UNCIALS AND HALF-UNCIALS

It was probably Patrick who first brought the Roman alphabet to Ireland. Uncial letters had already been developed in Rome from the original neat Latin alphabet. Because of the ease of writing with a quill or metal pen on parchment, the letters had lost much of their straightness and had developed curves.

From the uncial was developed the simple and beautiful half-uncial, which made no attempt to hide the fact that it was written with a quill pen.

THE BOOK OF KELLS

As Christianity spread throughout Ireland, monks began to copy the Bible and other religious writings. An example of their work is the Book of Kells, considered by many to be the most beautiful book ever produced. Such books were usually highly decorated and often contained pictures painted in colours.

Working by themselves, away from the rest of Europe, the Irish monks developed their own style of writing, a "book hand" of great beauty.

AUGUSTINE IN ENGLAND

It was probably Augustine, an Italian missionary, who brought the Roman alphabet back to England, where he was aided by Irish monks. The alphabet had once been introduced by the Romans, but their civilization had all but disappeared from Britain during the onslaughts of tribes from northern Europe.

ROMAN LETTERS IN ENGLAND

When the alphabet first spread to northern Europe, it contained only capital letters. How then did the small letters come into being? And when did the alphabet first reach England?

A page from the Book of Kells ⟶

54

55

The Caroline alphabet. Note that the v has become
rounded into a u. The reason for this is given on page 59.

A monk copying a manuscript. The knife in his left hand
is used for erasing errors.

abcdefghiklm
nopqrſtuxyz

CHARLEMAGNE

Gradually, over a period of a few centuries, the Roman Empire began to fall apart under the attacks of barbarian tribes. In the eighth century, Charlemagne, King of the Frankish tribes who lived along the Rhine River, brought a large part of the former Roman Empire under his rule.

Because he was eager to restore learning in his domain, Charlemagne invited an English scholar named Alcuin to start a palace school at Tours, in what is now France.

ALCUIN AND THE CAROLINE ALPHABET

Alcuin was also given the task of rewriting all Church literature. To accomplish this task, he taught the monks in his schools the beautiful method of writing used by the Irish and English monks of that period. As time passed, he developed a style of writing which eventually led to the formation of the small letters in use today. They were called *Caroline minuscules,* or small letters.

Until that time, large capital letters had been used merely to decorate the beginning of a page or paragraph. Alcuin changed this by making the first letter of every sentence a capital. He also introduced the use of punctuation, sentences, and paragraphs.

At that time, few people were educated. Even Charlemagne, the great King, had to employ others to write his letters and to read for him, for he had never been taught to do either for himself. Learning was kept alive by the monks.

HANDWRITTEN BOOKS

But copying in the monasteries must have been uncomfortable work in winter. Often, fires were not permitted in the rooms where the monks were writing, lest the precious books and parchment sheets be accidentally burned.

Most of the copying was done by monks called *scribes.* But other persons, called *rubricators,* put in titles and headlines, and decorated the borders.

This old manuscript is bound in leather over thin boards.

57

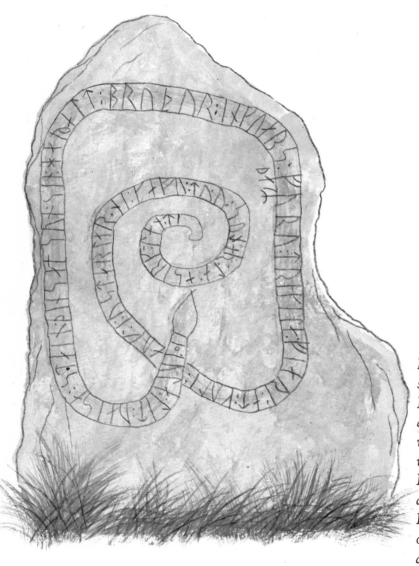

Left: A rune stone. Such stones may still be seen in Sweden, Denmark, Norway, and the British Isles. This form of writing was used as late as the 17th century and appeared mostly on tombstones. Some scholars believe it was borrowed from the Etruscans.
Below: The line of scratches is actually another form of writing found in the British Isles. It too is very old, although, since it often appeared side by side with the Roman alphabet, it is probably not as old as runes. This form of writing is called ogham and was often used by the Celts for secret messages.

Three New Letters

During the Middle Ages, three letters were introduced which were unknown to the Romans—J, U, and W. Each of them came into the alphabet at a different time and in a different way.

The Romans did not use the W, and so when the alphabet was brought to England a sign was needed for that sound, for which the English had been using a symbol called a *wen*. This letter came from the Runic alphabet, a writing system used in Britain before the introduction of the Roman alphabet.

V and U

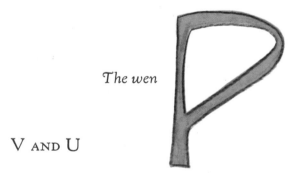

The wen

A wen looked something like our small letter p. It remained a part of the English alphabet until the coming of the Normans, who crossed the English Channel from their home in Normandy in France and conquered England in A.D. 1066.

Since the language of the Normans was not English, their pronunciation of W was different from that of the English. The Norman's was a somewhat double sound, and so they used one U for the first sound and another for the second. When written as a single symbol, it was a UU— a "double u", as we still call it.

As for the U, the Romans had employed the letter V for the sounds of both V and U. At first the English did the same thing, but gradually, as with many of the Roman letters when written as minuscules, the form changed and the sharp point of the V disappeared. The letter then looked like our U. Alcuin returned the pointed V to the alphabet as a capital letter, but he continued the use of the U for the minuscule.

Since there were now two sounds for this letter, English printers began using a capital U and a minuscule u for the U sound, adding a new letter to our alphabet. For the V sound, a capital V with a minuscule v were used.

I and J

In the minuscules the letter i, which was undotted, was often confusing. When two 'i's appeared side by side, they looked like a u. It was then that some clever scribes thought of putting over the i a small dash, which later became a dot.

Other scribes, in order to avoid confusing two 'i's with the u, began to put a long tail on the second i, which then looked like our j. This custom was continued for many years.

Originally the Romans had used the symbol I for two sounds. For example, they pronounced *Iulius* as *Yoo-lee-us,* the first i sounding like our y in *your,* and the second i sounding like *ee*. In 1600 the Spaniards began to use I for one of these sounds and the J for the other. We now write *Iulius* as *Julius.*

Paper

Before the invention of printing, books written by the monks were rare and very precious because it took so long to copy them. Sometimes a monk spent his entire life working on a single book. At the beginning of the 13th century, one of the richest libraries in western Europe contained only 150 volumes.

Because books were so rare, education was limited to monks and to the sons of the rich. Two inventions helped change this: the development of papermaking and the invention of printing.

PARCHMENT AND PAPYRUS

The writing material most common in Europe before the 14th century was parchment, which, as we know, was made from animal skins. But there were never enough skins to supply the scribes.

Papyrus was also used, but it too had drawbacks. First, it was a rather fragile material that could not withstand dampness. Also, it was somewhat hard to obtain in Europe since the papyrus plant did not grow there. A new material was needed, but one had been in existence, unknown to Europeans, for centuries. This was paper.

Paper: A Chinese Invention

Paper was first made in China about A.D. 100, but the Chinese were able to keep the process hidden from other nations for more than six centuries. Then, in 751, China's secret was discovered by the Arabs, who proceeded to open their own mills and start their own manufacture. The first European paper mill began to operate towards the end of the 13th century.

Papermaking

At that time linen rags were the raw materials of papermaking. After the rags were soaked, they were put into a vat and beaten to a pulp. When a sieve of fine wire mounted in a wooden frame was dipped into the vat, the wire screen was covered with a thin layer of pulp.

The sieve was then placed on a slanted surface to permit the water to drain. When the sieve was turned upside down, the thin sheet of pulp dropped onto a layer of felt which absorbed more of the moisture.

Another piece of felt was put on top of the first, and a second sheet of drying pulp was placed upon it. When a hundred sheets were in the pile, it was pressed to squeeze out more water. After the sheets were dried in a special room, they were ready for use.

Since flax, the plant used in making linen, grew well in Europe, rags for papermaking were easy to come by and cheap.

The Advantages of Paper

Paper was a satisfactory medium for those who wrote with pen or brush because ink did not spread on the paper as it did on papyrus. In addition paper was a stronger, tougher material.

Parchment provided a good writing surface too, but as we have seen it was expensive and too scarce to satisfy the increased demand that followed the invention of printing. It was also too thick and stiff to be used for printing, but paper was plentiful, cheap, light, and easy to use. Although some fine papers are still made of rags, most of the paper in common use today is made of wood pulp.

Flax plants from which linen is made

The Invention of Printing

PRINTING IN CHINA

Printing was another invention of the Chinese. The oldest known book was printed in China in A.D. 868, almost six centuries before Gutenberg invented movable type in Germany.

The Chinese book of A.D. 868 contained six pages of text and one picture. Each page was printed from a single block of wood, in a mirror image. This means that the characters on the block looked as they would in a mirror. For example, an E would look like Ǝ.

After the characters for the page had been drawn on a wooden block, everything that was not to be printed was cut away. Ink was then put on this surface and a sheet of parchment was pressed down upon it. When the parchment was removed, it was imprinted with the characters from the block.

Johann Gutenberg

CHINESE MOVABLE TYPE

A few hundred years later, the Chinese carried printing a step further by cutting small individual characters from wood. These could be moved about on a base, and used over and over again.

It would seem that after such an invention books would have been printed regularly in China. But this was not so; there were too many characters in the Chinese writing system to make printing practical.

Because news of the Chinese use of printing did not reach Europe until long after Gutenberg had done his work, he is given the credit for the invention of movable type. He worked out his idea completely alone in the year 1454.

GUTENBERG'S INVENTION

Gutenberg's printing method was an improvement over what the Chinese had done. They had made their type of wood, which didn't last long because of its softness. Gutenberg's type was made of an alloy, a mixture of various metals. It was therefore much harder than wooden type and lasted a longer time.

INKS FOR PRINTING

To ink type, the Chinese used a water colour, but this gave a very uneven character to their printing. For his ink, Gutenberg employed a thicker, stickier paint used by artists, and quite similar to today's printing inks.

Another improvement introduced by Gutenberg was the use of a wine press to put even pressure on the paper during the actual printing.

When he first started out as a printer, Gutenberg made books as the early Chinese had made

Gutenberg reading a page that has just been printed. The printer at the right is standing at a press.

them—by cutting on a single block all the type that was to appear on a single page. But he soon realised that printing could be speeded up if each letter were a separate piece of type. Many such pieces could be put together to spell out anything that was wanted on a single page. After the page had been printed, the type could be removed, cleaned, and used again and again.

Gutenberg worked on his idea for many years. It was perfected in 1454 and in the next 35 years its use spread throughout Europe. The invention reached England in 1476.

WANDERING PRINTERS

Much of the credit for carrying the new printing method throughout Europe can be given to wandering printers who roamed from place to place, carrying with them their tools and sometimes even their type.

With the coming of movable type, one printer could do the work of 25 monks. Although the handwritten books had been beautiful, printed books were cheaper and available to a much greater number of readers.

Italic Type

Among the first people to use the new printing method outside Germany were the Italians, and Italy became for many years the centre of the printing trade. It was Aldus Manutius, a Venetian printer, who developed a type face which we know as Italic. It is still in use today. *This sentence is printed in Italic type.*

Other than Manutius' one new look in letters, the letters used by present-day printers are quite similar to those used in Gutenberg's time.

The Steam-Powered Press

Printing continued to be done in much the same way for well over 350 years. Then early in the 19th century, a press, powered by steam, was built in England by a German engineer named Friedrich Koenig. Previously, printers had been able to turn out about 250 sheets of printed matter in an hour. Koenig's press made possible the printing of 1100 sheets in the same period of time, but presses today can print more than 50 times that number in an hour.

Offset Printing

After the use of steam to power presses, changes in printing have been mainly attempts to print faster. But an important change of another kind was the development of offset printing. Many things are printed today by this method, which permits the printing in four colours on both sides of the paper, all in one operation.

No major changes have been made in writing since the time of Johann Gutenberg. However, radio, motion pictures, television, and tape recordings may bring about a change in communications that will be as important as the invention of movable type.

Talking Books

Already people are sending voice letters to one another. Many libraries circulate voice recordings to help in the learning of foreign languages. More and more schools are using such machines in teaching students, and recordings of books have been used by the blind for many years.

It is possible that in the near future libraries will have large collections of books recorded on

An alphabet that is in use today

A B C D E F G

P Q R S T U V V

g h i j k l m n o p

tape, in addition to those now on library shelves. Some day people may be able to listen to books being read by their authors.

Already many readings of poetry are available on recordings made by the poets who wrote the verse. The poet's emphasis on certain words and phrases—even his pauses—can shed light on the meaning of his poems.

THE WONDER OF THE ALPHABET

Since the time, thousands and thousands of years ago, when primitive man began to use his brain to improve his life, human beings have wrought many wonders. But possibly the most wonderful of all was the discovery of writing as a means of communicating ideas. It was this discovery that led, over many centuries and through many lands, to the invention of the Roman alphabet.

In the beginning, writing was probably used to send messages and to keep records. But man, who has a great need to express himself in some form of art, found that writing could be used to tell stories and to put down thoughts about the world around him. But he needed a consistent way of communicating these stories and ideas, so that he could be understood by other people. The invention of the alphabet made it easier for him to write down his thoughts. People who used the same alphabet could then read and understand what he had written.

THE IMPORTANCE OF THE PRINTING PRESS

But man still had difficulty in circulating his ideas. The process of copying manuscripts was long and tedious, and the number of books available was limited. The invention of the printing press solved this problem. Many books could be printed quickly and inexpensively and made available to the common people.

Today, using the alphabet, anyone may write down his ideas. If they are important or interesting enough to be published, they can then be passed on from one person to another and be shared by the people of many countries and by those of centuries to come.

So, in a real sense, the first primitive man who made scratches on bone or rock was opening the way to the search for knowledge which has made it possible for a man to walk on the moon.

H I J K L M N O

X Y Z a b c d e f

q r s t u v w x y z

Hebrew is still studied by many American Jews, particularly those who belong to Orthodox Judaism. It is written and read from right to left, and its first two letters are Aleph and Beth.

Another important alphabet used today is the Greek, shown below. According to an old legend, a man named Cadmus, of the city of Thebes, first brought the Greek alphabet from Phoenicia 3500 years ago. However, scholars believe that it has existed in Greece for only 2800 years.

The Greek alphabet was passed on to the Etruscans; from them it reached the Romans, through whom it has come down to us. Another variation of this alphabet was adapted by a bishop named Ulfilas for the use of the Goths. However, Gothic letters disappeared from use when the Goths were absorbed into the Roman Empire.

The Greek alphabet is important to us —
because from it the Romans borrowed to
develop their beautiful letters. Here is
the Greek alphabet in use today.

Some Other Alphabets

HEBREW, GREEK AND RUSSIAN

This book has been mainly concerned with the Roman alphabet—the one we use. However, there are about 50 other alphabets still being written and read in other parts of the world.

Among them is the Hebrew shown above. The Hebrew language, and its alphabet, were derived from Aramaic, an ancient Semitic tongue which was spoken by Jesus. Aramaic spread throughout the Arab countries of North Africa, into Turkey, through the Middle East, and as far south as India.

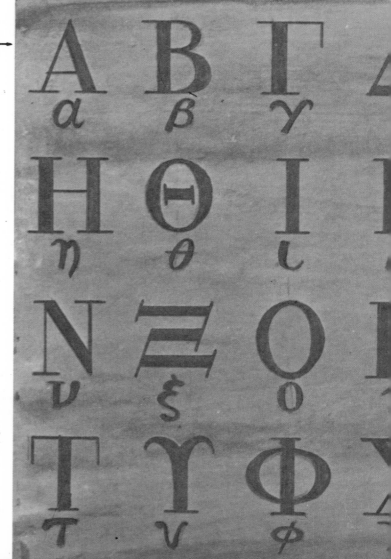

The Russian alphabet. Although some of these letters look like our own, they are not derived from the Roman alphabet. The Russians borrowed from the Greeks, as did the Romans.

Today American college fraternities and sororities use Greek letters to designate their organizations.

Above is the Russian alphabet. It was first devised in the 9th century by Cyril and Methodius, two bishops of Constantinople who brought Christianity to the Slavs. Cyril and Methodius started with the Greek alphabet and used many Greek characters. But new symbols were needed for Slavic sounds which did not occur in Greek. A few were borrowed from the Hebrew, the rest they devised themselves.

The alphabet invented by the Slavs is called Cyrillic. It is used by those people who followed the Eastern Church: the Russians, the Bulgars, the Serbs, and the Ukrainians. The Slavic peoples who belong to the Roman Catholic Church use the Roman alphabet.

67

The Arabic alphabet, like Hebrew, is written from right to left. Pictured here is a plate from an Arabic manuscript probably printed around A.D. 1475. It illustrates the story of Rustam who had gone out to battle the evil spirit Ahriman. Rustam is sleeping while his horse protects him from a lion.

ACKNOWLEDGMENTS The editor and publisher have made every effort to trace the ownership of all copyrighted material and to secure permission from holders of such material. In the event of any question arising as to the use of any material, the publisher and editor, while expressing regret for inadvertent error, will be pleased to make the necessary corrections in future printings. Thanks are due to the following publishers and universities for permission to use the material indicated.

Fernand Hazan for material adapted from ETRUSCAN ART by M. F. Briguet

Iris Verlag for material adapted from PERSIAN PAINTING; selection from the collection of Sir Bernard Eckstein

Albert Skira, Editions d'Art, for material adapted from EGYPTIAN PAINTING

Trinity College, University of Dublin, for material adapted from the Book of Kells

The University of Chicago Press for material adapted from THEY WROTE ON CLAY by Edward Chiera, copyright © 1938, 1969 by The University of Chicago

Yale University for material adapted from an article about Alexander Marshak